PRETEEN PRESSURES

DRUG ABUSE

by Suzanne J. Murdico

RSVP

**RAINTREE
STECK-VAUGHN**
P U B L I S H E R S
The Steck-Vaughn Company

Austin, Texas

Consultants
John Mariani, Social Worker, Family Service Association of Bucks County, PA
William B. Presnell, Clinical Member, American Association for Marriage and Family Therapy

Developed for Steck-Vaughn Company by
Visual Education Corporation, Princeton, New Jersey
Project Director: Jewel Moulthrop
Editor: Paula McGuire
Editorial Assistant: Jacqueline Morais
Photo Research: Sara Matthews
Electronic Preparation: Cynthia C. Feldner, Manager; Fiona Torphy
Production Supervisor: Ellen Foos
Electronic Production: Lisa Evans-Skopas, Manager; Elise Dodeles, Deirdre Sheean, Isabelle Verret
Interior Design: Maxson Crandall

Raintree Steck-Vaughn Publishers staff
Editor: Kathy DeVico
Project Manager: Joyce Spicer

Photo Credits: Cover: © David Young-Wolff/PhotoEdit; 6: © David Young-Wolff/PhotoEdit; 14: © Tony Freeman/PhotoEdit; 17: © Mary Kate Denny/PhotoEdit; 20: © David Young-Wolff/PhotoEdit; 22: © The Kobal Collection; 25: © Michael Newman/PhotoEdit; 28: © David Young-Wolff/PhotoEdit; 31: © Tony Freeman/PhotoEdit; 36: © Demmie Todd/Walt Disney Pictures; 38: © Michael Newman/PhotoEdit; 42: © David Young-Wolff/PhotoEdit

Library of Congress Cataloging-in-Publication Data
Murdico, Suzanne J.
     Drug abuse/by Suzanne J. Murdico.
        p.   cm. — (Preteen pressures)
     Includes bibliographical references and index.
     Summary: Describes the dangers of drugs and provides information about getting help for substance abuse problems.
     ISBN 0-8172-5027-1
     1. Drug abuse—United States—Prevention—Juvenile literature. 2. Preteens—Drug use—United States—Juvenile literature. [1. Drug abuse.] I. Title. II. Series.
HV5825.M79 1998
362.29'17'0973—dc21   97-29235
                                                        CIP
                                                        AC

Printed and bound in the United States
1 2 3 4 5 6 7 8 9 0 LB 01 00 99 98 97

CONTENTS

INTRODUCTION

Drug abuse is one of the worst problems in the United States today. It affects people of all ages, races, and income levels. Drug abuse occurs in cities, suburbs, and rural areas. Drug abusers may be parents, children, brothers, aunts, friends, neighbors, or classmates. Whether or not you know someone who uses drugs, drug abuse affects all of us. Here are some of the facts:

▶ Nearly 450,000 Americans die each year as a result of smoking cigarettes.

▶ In the United States, secondhand smoke causes about 3,000 lung cancer deaths of nonsmokers each year.

▶ The use of alcohol plays a key role in nearly 70 percent of manslaughters and more than 60 percent of assaults.

▶ In 1993, 40 percent of the deaths of 15- to 20-year-olds in traffic accidents were alcohol related.

▶ In 1994 more than half of the new cases of HIV infection (the virus that causes AIDS) were related to drug use.

▶ In a study of young people who attempted suicide, 70 percent frequently used alcohol or other drugs.

▶ In 1995 more than 142,000 hospital emergency room incidents were related to cocaine use.

Sources: *Tips for Teens: Smoking,* Substance Abuse and Mental Health Services Administration (SAMHSA) (1997); *Making the Link: Violence & Alcohol,* National Clearinghouse for Alcohol and Drug Information (NCADI) (1997); DAWN Survey, NCADI (1996).

Drug use often begins at a young age. The majority of adult users began taking drugs when they were teens or preteens. Studies show that the younger people are when they start using drugs, the more serious their drug problems are likely to become. Young people who are just experimenting with cigarettes or alcohol often become hooked on them. People who start smoking cigarettes in their teens are 100 times more likely to smoke marijuana. They are also more likely to try other illegal drugs, such as cocaine and heroin.

You may feel that the drug problem is overwhelming and that there is nothing you can do about it. But there are ways that you can help. The most important way is not to use drugs. Don't try them—not even once. By saying no to drugs, you will not only help yourself, but may also encourage others to do the same.

Another way to help is by learning all you can about different kinds of drugs and their effects. This book will provide you with the information you need to understand drug abuse and the problems it causes. Once you understand why drugs are dangerous, you should be persuaded to stay away from them. And you will have some hard facts to share with your friends. Together you can fight the war against all drug abuse.

Drugs come in all forms—legal and illegal—but the consequences of abusing them can be equally damaging.

TYPES OF DRUGS

A drug is a chemical substance that alters the way your body works and sometimes the way you think or act. When prescribed by a physician, drugs (or medications) can cure or improve a medical condition. Some drugs, however, whether or not they are prescription drugs, are used by people to make themselves feel better or to help them avoid unpleasant feelings. And a wide variety of drugs, many of them illegal, is available today. These drugs come in many forms—pills, powders, and liquids—and they are used in many ways.

Drugs usually enter the body in one of three ways:

▶ They are ingested—taken orally, or swallowed by mouth.

▶ They are inhaled—breathed in through the nose or mouth.

▶ They are injected—taken by needle and released directly into the bloodstream.

Almost all drugs have side effects. Side effects are unwanted reactions that occur in some people when drugs are taken in normal doses. Side effects may be short-term or long-term. The short-term effects might include headache or nausea, and they usually go away within a few hours after the person stops taking the drug.

The long-term effects develop over time and may be permanent. Long-term effects include damage to the brain, liver, and kidneys. Most long-term effects never go away, even if a person stops using the drug. Learning about the side effects of drugs will help you understand why you should avoid them.

TOBACCO

Tia's father has smoked cigarettes for many years. One day, when her father was at work, Tia decided to try a cigarette. With her first puff, she started coughing and her throat burned. After a few more puffs, she felt dizzy and sick to her stomach. If cigarettes make you feel so bad, Tia wondered, why does my father smoke them?

Millions of people, including Tia's father, probably disliked their first cigarette. But, perhaps because of peer pressure or a desire to look "cool," they continued to smoke. Now they are addicted to, or dependent on, cigarettes. Because tobacco is legal for adults to buy and use, you may not think of cigarettes as a drug. However, the tobacco in cigarettes contains a powerful and addictive drug called nicotine. In addition, cigarette smoke contains about 4,000 chemicals, including 200 poisons. Not all tobacco is smoked. Some people use smokeless tobacco, which is either chewed or held in the mouth. Smokeless tobacco also contains nicotine.

Many risks are associated with tobacco use. Smoking cigarettes causes frequent colds and coughs, a reduced sense of smell and taste, premature wrinkles, and an increase in heart rate and blood pressure.

Long-term smoking can cause stomach ulcers, heart disease, stroke, emphysema (a lung disease), and some forms of cancer. For young people, smoking cigarettes is especially harmful. Your body is still growing, and some of the chemicals in tobacco products can have a damaging effect on this process.

MARIJUANA

Brianna's older brother, Justin, smokes marijuana all the time. He has pressured Brianna to try it, but she always says no. She doesn't like the way Justin acts when he has been smoking marijuana. He laughs for no apparent reason and stumbles around looking stupid. Then he eats all the junk food he can find in the house. Why would Brianna want to act like that?

Of all the illegal drugs used in America today, marijuana is probably the most common. It comes from the dried leaves of the hemp plant. Similar to tobacco, marijuana is rolled into cigarettes and smoked. The short-term effects of marijuana use include decrease in memory, difficulty in thinking and problem solving, and loss of coordination. People who smoke marijuana may also experience an increased heart rate and feelings of anxiety.

Smoking marijuana has some of the same long-term effects as smoking cigarettes. Marijuana smoke contains some of the same cancer-causing chemicals found in tobacco smoke. People who use marijuana regularly suffer from frequent coughs and from lung problems, such as bronchitis and emphysema. Marijuana may also affect the reproductive and immune systems.

ALCOHOL

Although alcohol is legal for adults to buy and use, it is still a potentially dangerous drug. While at first alcohol gives a person a feeling of well-being, it is a depressant drug. That means that it slows down the functioning of the brain, making it difficult for drinkers to think clearly. Alcohol also makes drinkers clumsy and slows down their reaction time. For these reasons, a person who has been drinking alcohol should never try to drive a car. Heavy drinking over an extended time can cause serious liver damage and even death.

INHALANTS

One Saturday night Alex went to a party at a friend's house. Some of the kids were using inhalants. Alex watched as they poured paint thinner onto a rag and held the rag to their faces. One of them handed the rag to Alex and told him to try it. He did, but something went terribly wrong. Within a few minutes, he fell to the floor. The other kids shook him and shook him. When he wouldn't wake up, they called 911. The ambulance arrived quickly, but Alex was already dead.

Inhalants are chemical fumes that are inhaled to produce mind-altering effects. They are extremely dangerous drugs. Surprisingly, inhalants are available in many places, such as grocery and hardware stores. Most are fairly cheap and can be purchased legally. How can these deadly drugs be so easy to obtain? The reason is that inhalants are usually household products, such as glue, spray paint, cleaning fluids, and gasoline.

These products, sniffed through the nose or mouth, go directly into the lungs. Common side effects of inhalants include nausea, vomiting, headache, slurred speech, and loss of motor skills. Long-term effects of inhalant use include serious health problems, such as damage to the brain, kidneys, liver, and nervous system. And as in Alex's case, even one-time use of inhalants can cause heart failure and death.

STIMULANTS

Stimulants are sometimes called "uppers." As you might guess, people take these drugs to make themselves feel "up," or energetic. Stimulants provide a temporary feeling of energy and limitless power. But this feeling lasts for only a matter of minutes. Then users feel depressed, edgy, and irritable. They also crave more of the drug.

Some types of mild stimulants are found in food and other products. Caffeine is a stimulant found in coffee, tea, and some soft drinks. Nicotine, which is found in tobacco products, is also a stimulant. Too much caffeine or nicotine can cause sleeplessness and nervousness. Some stimulants, however, are strong, dangerous, and generally illegal. Cocaine, crack, and amphetamines are stimulants in this category.

Cocaine and Crack

Cocaine is a white powder that comes from coca leaves. The coca plant grows in South America. This drug is generally inhaled through the nose or injected with a needle. Crack is a form of cocaine that is smoked.

Both cocaine and crack are very dangerous. These drugs carry serious physical risks. They can cause death even the first time people use them. Any amount of cocaine or crack can cause an increase in heart rate, breathing rate, blood pressure, and body temperature. Use of these drugs can cause brain seizures, heart attacks, strokes, and respiratory failure. All of these conditions may be fatal. And because each person's body is different, there is no way to tell who is most likely to have a severe reaction to these drugs.

Use of cocaine and crack also poses psychological risks. A user's behavior may become violent and unpredictable. Users may feel anxious, confused, and depressed. They may also lose interest in family, friends, hobbies, and other activities. Some users even lose touch with reality.

Amphetamines

Many amphetamines are available in pill form and are taken by mouth. Some are injected into a vein. One type of amphetamine—commonly known as "ice" or "crystal"—is smoked. Use of amphetamines produces effects that are similar to those of cocaine. They last longer, however.

Regular use of amphetamines causes many serious side effects. Amphetamines affect the central nervous system and may cause tremors, convulsions, and even death. In addition, they can cause strokes and heart problems. Users may become overly suspicious. Their behavior may become violent and unpredictable. Sometimes they see things that don't really exist.

DEPRESSANTS

Depressants, which are sometimes called "downers," are the opposite of stimulants. When taken in moderate doses, these drugs produce effects that are very similar to those caused by alcohol. The side effects include slurred speech, impaired judgment, and loss of coordination. With regular use of depressants, a person needs more and more of the drug to achieve the same effect. This leads to an increased risk of accidental overdose.

NARCOTICS

People take narcotics, such as heroin, to achieve a sense of well-being and calmness. Narcotics, which make users feel less tense and anxious, come in several forms. Some are taken orally or are injected with a needle. Others are smoked or inhaled.

Many factors affect the way users react to narcotics. These factors include the amount of the drug, how the drug was taken, and whether the person has used the drug before. Along with the desired effects of reduced anxiety, narcotics have many unwanted side effects. Users may feel sleepy, have trouble concentrating, and experience nausea and vomiting. Over time, users need more of the drug to achieve the desired effects.

ANABOLIC STEROIDS

Ben loves to play football and wants to try out for the school team. But when he compares himself to the other kids, he feels little and scrawny. The other day he heard

Steroids may build up muscles, but the dangers of steroid use greatly outweigh the benefits.

some of the football players talking about "bulking up" with steroids. Ben decided that he would try steroids. Maybe they could help him develop bigger muscles so that he would look more like the other players.

If Ben knew more about steroids, he would probably decide not to use them. Anabolic steroids are drugs that contain a substance similar to testosterone, which is a male hormone. They are taken by mouth or are injected into the muscles. Because steroids promote muscle growth and strength, they are most commonly abused by athletes. Some athletes take these drugs in an effort to improve their performance and to enhance their physical appearance.

Short-term effects of steroids include high blood pressure and cholesterol levels, severe acne, and trembling. In addition, males who use steroids may lose their hair, develop breasts, and experience shrinking of the testicles. In females, steroid use causes masculine traits to develop. Females may grow facial hair, their voices may deepen, and their menstrual cycles may become irregular.

The long-term effects of steroids are not yet known. However, evidence suggests that these drugs can damage the heart, liver, and reproductive organs. Steroids can create additional problems for young people because they can damage the growth areas on the ends of bones. This damage can cause stunted growth.

HALLUCINOGENS

Hallucinogens affect the user's perception of reality. These drugs are called hallucinogens because they cause users to hallucinate. That means seeing objects or hearing sounds that don't really exist. Some of the best-known hallucinogens are lysergic acid diethylamide (LSD), phencyclidine (PCP), psilocybin ("magic mushrooms"), peyote, and mescaline.

The physical effects of hallucinogens include an increase in heart rate and blood pressure, lack of muscular coordination, sleeplessness, and tremors. Hallucinogens may also cause coma, convulsions, and heart and lung failure. Because users become less aware of touch and pain, they sometimes injure themselves.

Many psychological risks are associated with hallucinogens. Users may feel anxious, depressed, overly suspicious, confused, and out of control. Hallucinogens often cause people to behave violently toward others. Weeks or months after using hallucinogens, some people have flashbacks—partial visions of a previous drug experience. The effects of hallucinogens vary from person to person and from use to use. There is no way to predict whether the experience will be enjoyable or extremely frightening.

DRUGS AS MEDICATION

Not all drugs are bad for you. Some drugs can help you become well if you are sick. These drugs are usually referred to as medication. If you ever had an ear infection, for example, the doctor may have given you antibiotics to help you recover. You may have a friend or classmate who is diabetic and takes insulin. Perhaps one of your parents takes medication for high blood pressure. Even aspirin and cough syrup are drugs.

Some medications, such as those for headaches and colds, are available over the counter. These drugs are found at pharmacies and grocery stores, and anyone can buy them. Over-the-counter medications are not usually very strong. Other medications are available only with a doctor's prescription. Drugs used as medication are meant to help people. But even prescription drugs can be harmful if used incorrectly.

Jesse started taking prescription medication to dull the pain of a toothache. He liked the way the pills made

Prescription medication may be helpful to one person, but dangerous to another if used incorrectly.

him feel, so he kept taking them even after his tooth stopped hurting. Keesha was having trouble falling asleep. She started taking prescription sleeping pills that she found in her mother's medicine cabinet. Although Jesse and Keesha are taking legal drugs, they are not following a doctor's instructions. Both are guilty of drug abuse.

WHY PEOPLE USE DRUGS

How much do you really know about drugs? You may have heard some things from your friends. But how much of what you heard is really true? You may be surprised by some of the facts below.

MYTH: Smoking cigarettes will calm me down.

FACT: Nicotine, the drug in tobacco, is a stimulant. Smoking cigarettes increases your heart rate and can make you feel nervous and edgy.

MYTH: Nothing can happen to me the first time I try a drug.

FACT: Trying some drugs even once can make you very sick or even kill you.

MYTH: My drug use affects only me.

FACT: Your drug use affects all of the people around you, including your parents, brothers and sisters, friends, and classmates.

MYTH: I can buy glue and paint thinner at the store, so they must be safe to inhale.

FACT: Glue and paint thinner are not meant to be inhaled. Using them in a way other than the way the manufacturer intended is extremely dangerous.

MYTH: I don't use drugs every day, so I don't have a problem.

FACT: If you use drugs often, even if it's not every day, you have a problem. Even if you use drugs only occasionally, you are likely to develop a problem in the future.

DEALING WITH PROBLEMS

Adolescence can be a difficult time. Your body is growing and changing. Your emotions may run hot and cold. One minute you may be happy, and the next you may feel like crying or screaming. You have more responsibilities than you did when you were younger. And people expect more of you than ever before. Some young people become overwhelmed by all of these changes. Urged on by their peers, some try drugs. The drugs seem to make their problems disappear, and they start to rely on the drugs to make themselves feel better.

Nicole's parents argue a lot. Nicole usually stays in her room and plays her CDs so that she can't hear the yelling. She's afraid that her parents are headed for divorce. Recently Nicole has been spending a lot of time at her friend Allison's house. Allison smokes marijuana, and Nicole tried it. Smoking marijuana makes Nicole forget about her problems for a little while. Of course, her problems are still there when she goes home.

Ramon and Paul have been best friends since kindergarten. They used to spend a lot of time together, playing basketball and street hockey, riding their bikes, and playing computer games. A few months ago, Paul moved away. Now Ramon is bored all the time. He never knows what to do with his free time. The other day Ramon heard a few kids at school talking about sniffing glue. Ramon decided that he would try it, too, just for kicks.

Both Nicole and Ramon think that drugs will make their problems go away. Using drugs may take their minds off their problems for a little while. But sooner or later, they will have to deal with them. In addition, drugs usually make a bad situation worse. Drugs often cause people to do and say things that they wouldn't normally do or say. This often leads to arguments. And people who are caught using drugs get into trouble with parents, teachers, and the police.

Drugs are never the only solution to a boring day. Bright, creative, healthy young people know how to have fun without drugs.

FINDING SOLUTIONS

Drugs are not the answer to your problems. There are much better solutions to any problem you may face. Here are some common problems faced by young people and a few solutions for each.

PROBLEM: I'm bored. There's nothing to do around here.

SOLUTIONS:

▶ Join a school club.
▶ Volunteer at a hospital or animal shelter.
▶ Take up a new hobby or sport.
▶ Start a daily exercise program.

PROBLEM: Everyone else uses drugs. I want to be cool.

SOLUTIONS:

▶ Find friends who don't use drugs.
▶ Decide to be different.
▶ Start a club in which all members agree not to use drugs.

PROBLEM: My parents are driving me crazy!

SOLUTIONS:

▶ Sit down with your parents and discuss the situation.
▶ Take part in activities outside your home, such as sports, volunteer work, or community programs.

PROBLEM: I like taking risks. Drugs seem exciting, so I think I'll try them.

SOLUTIONS:

▶ Take a physical risk by learning a new sport or joining a team.
▶ Take a social risk by introducing yourself to someone you don't know.
▶ Take an emotional risk by sharing your feelings.

The Story of
River Phoenix

It's hard to understand why some people choose to abuse drugs. On the surface, they may not seem to have any problems. But beneath the surface, something may be troubling them.

River Phoenix was a person like that. He seemed to have it all. He was young, handsome, talented, rich, and famous. River was a popular actor who starred in more than a dozen movies. Thousands of fans adored him, and he was often written about in teen magazines. Many people thought that he would have a long and successful career as a movie star. Instead, River Phoenix died at the age of 23—the result of a drug overdose.

With his career on the rise, River Phoenix had a lot to live for.

The oldest of five children, River was born in 1970. He began his acting career as a teenager and appeared in his first major film when he was only 15. Right away people noticed his talent. At the age of 18, River was nominated for an Academy Award—one of the greatest honors given to movie actors. He starred in several other movies and was considered one of Hollywood's most gifted young actors.

In the early morning hours of October 31, 1993, River was hanging out at a Los Angeles nightclub. Suddenly he said that he didn't feel well, and he ran outside. His friends followed him and found River lying on the sidewalk. He was having convulsions—violent, uncontrolled body movements. While River's girlfriend tried desperately to help him, his brother called 911. Their efforts were of no use. River Phoenix died a short while later. His death was caused by an overdose of cocaine, morphine, and other drugs.

River's fans were shocked and upset by the young actor's death. During the next few days, they placed flowers, candles, and notes on the sidewalk where he died. Many people had trouble believing that River took drugs. He was a strict vegetarian who seemed concerned about taking care of his body. How could someone like this abuse drugs? Maybe the pressures of fame were too much for him. Or maybe he simply fell in with the wrong crowd.

We will probably never fully understand why River Phoenix abused drugs. Sadly, he didn't live long enough to tell us.

HOW DRUG ABUSE AFFECTS THE USER

> **66** January 24
> Anyone who says pot and acid are not addicting is a damn, stupid, raving idiot, unenlightened fool! I've been on them since July 10, and when I've been off I've been scared to death to even think of anything that even looks or seems like dope. All the time pretending to myself that I could take it or leave it! **99**

This quote is from *Go Ask Alice*, the real diary of a teenage drug user. She later died of a drug overdose. Although her words may seem very harsh, she is speaking from the viewpoint of someone who is addicted to drugs. What exactly do we mean when we say that someone has an addiction?

WHAT IS ADDICTION?

Addiction is a physical or psychological need for something. When people have a physical dependence on a drug, their bodies need the drug just to function. When people have a psychological dependence, they believe that they need the drug to feel good.

People cannot predict how easily they may become addicted—their best bet is to avoid making that first mistake of trying a drug.

Some drugs are more likely to cause addiction than others. Stimulants, depressants, and narcotics are drugs that can quickly cause a physical addiction. People who drink alcohol or smoke marijuana can develop a physical or psychological dependence on these drugs.

Some people are more prone to addiction than others. And drugs affect different people in different ways. One person may be able to smoke a few cigarettes a week for a long time and not become addicted. Another person may become addicted after smoking only a few cigarettes in a short time.

TOLERANCE AND WITHDRAWAL

Alcohol and marijuana are often called "gateway drugs." That is because the use of these drugs often opens the gate to other drugs. Many people who begin by thinking that they will just drink a small amount of alcohol or smoke a little marijuana become addicted. Over time, they need more and more of these drugs to achieve the same effects as they previously had with smaller amounts. In other words, their tolerance for drugs has increased. Eventually they need to use stronger drugs to achieve these effects.

When people become addicted to a drug, it is very difficult for them to stop using it. When they do stop, they go through withdrawal. Withdrawal consists of a series of symptoms that are physically and mentally painful. Depending on the drug, these symptoms can range from mild to severe. They include headaches, upset stomachs, shakiness, and panic attacks.

STAGES OF DRUG ABUSE

While each person's experience with drug use is different, some aspects may be common. Here is a typical story:

Age 10: Amanda's friend Kimberly thinks it's cool to smoke cigarettes. She encourages Amanda to try one. Soon Amanda is smoking four or five cigarettes a week.

Age 11: Amanda is addicted to cigarettes. She smokes whenever she can—sometimes eight or nine cigarettes a day.

Age 12: Amanda wants to feel more like an adult. Some older girls at school smoke marijuana. Amanda decides that she will seem more mature if she smokes marijuana, too.

Age 13: Amanda smokes marijuana several times a week. She cuts school a lot, and she is barely passing her classes. She has started stealing money from her mother's purse to pay for the marijuana.

Age 14: Amanda no longer feels the same "high" that she used to feel by smoking marijuana. She has started using cocaine.

Age 15: Amanda is addicted to cocaine. She has started selling drugs to support her habit.

Age 16: Amanda is arrested for cocaine possession. She must go through a drug rehabilitation program to stop using drugs, and she may have to go to a juvenile detention center.

SIGNS OF DRUG ABUSE

How can you tell if someone has a drug problem? It isn't always easy. Most people will lie about it or try to hide the problem. But there are some warning signs.

Someone you know may have a drug problem if he or she:

▶ Uses drugs or alcohol regularly
▶ Lies about the amount of alcohol or drugs used
▶ Thinks that drinking alcohol or using drugs is necessary to have a good time
▶ Often talks about drinking alcohol or using drugs

If a friend suddenly acts differently around you or no longer wants to do the same things you once enjoyed together, he or she may be using drugs.

- ▶ Spends time alone to drink or use drugs
- ▶ Experiences trouble with the police
- ▶ Misses school or work or performs poorly because of drug use
- ▶ Pressures other people to try drugs or alcohol
- ▶ Needs greater amounts of alcohol or other drugs to achieve the same effect as before
- ▶ No longer participates in activities that he or she used to enjoy with old friends

▶ Takes unnecessary risks, such as driving while under the influence of alcohol or other drugs

Anyone can have a drug problem. Maybe you are concerned about your own behavior. How can you tell if you have a problem with alcohol or other drugs? If you answer yes to one or more of the following questions, you may have a problem:

▶ Do you think that you need to drink alcohol or use drugs to have a good time?

▶ Do you have problems at school because of alcohol or drug use?

▶ Do you use drugs or alcohol to make yourself feel better after an unpleasant experience?

▶ Are you unable to predict whether or not you will drink alcohol or use drugs?

▶ Do you need larger amounts of drugs or alcohol to achieve the same effect that you used to have with smaller amounts?

▶ Do you drink alcohol or use drugs when you are by yourself?

▶ Do you promise that you won't use drugs or alcohol anymore, and then break those promises?

Source: *Just the Facts,* NCADI (1997).

HOW DRUG ABUSE AFFECTS OTHERS

The following quote is from the true story of Kelly, a 16-year-old drug addict, and his family. The passage shows how drug abuse affects more than just the user.

My son is a drug addict. . . . Kelly's addiction controlled our family like a tyrant for nearly two years. It still has a lot to do with how we spend our time. We spend two evenings a week in counseling sessions, we've been to our share of Narcotics Anonymous meetings, and we have written this book. Addiction can take hold in a matter of months; recovery in its various stages can take years.

From *Drugs and the Family* by Jo Martin and Kelly Clendenon (Chelsea House Publishers; Broomall, PA; 1988.)

A young person's addiction affects his or her parents, brothers and sisters, friends, and classmates. Similarly, a parent's drug addiction affects the other parent, children, coworkers, and friends. Drug abuse can tear apart families, end friendships, and destroy lives. Drug abuse also affects our society as a whole.

INJURIES

Because drugs affect the way a person's mind functions, drug users are more likely to be clumsy, react slowly, and make stupid mistakes. Consequently, drug users are more likely to injure themselves or others accidentally. People who drive while under the influence of alcohol, for example, are often involved in serious car accidents that injure or kill people. Some drugs cause users to become aggressive and to act violently. This may cause them to hurt themselves or others.

CRIME AND VIOLENCE

A strong link exists between drug use and crime and violence. In the United States, more than one-third of all arrests are for crimes related to alcohol and drug use. These crimes include driving while intoxicated, possession or use of illegal drugs, and drunkenness. In addition, many drug users commit crimes—such as robbery—to acquire money to pay for drugs.

Violent crimes include fights, assaults, child abuse, and rape. Many violent crimes are committed by people who are under the influence of alcohol or other drugs.

Crime, violence, and injuries occur more often when drugs are part of the picture.

Drug use often makes it difficult for a person to tell the difference between acceptable and unacceptable behavior. And some drugs, including alcohol, PCP, and steroids, may actually cause people to become violent.

Alcohol- and drug-related crimes cause terrible suffering and the loss of many lives. They also cost our society a great deal of money. Arresting people, bringing them to trial, and keeping them in jail are all very expensive.

SEX AND DRUG USE

Kyle and Heather are 15 years old and have been dating for several months. Kyle likes to take downers, and he talked Heather into trying them. Soon Kyle and Heather were popping pills whenever they were together. The drugs made them feel calm and relaxed. They hadn't planned to have sex. But one day, after taking downers, they just did it without thinking. They also didn't think about using a condom or other form of protection.

Now Heather is pregnant. A few days after she told Kyle, he stopped calling her. At school he pretends he doesn't see her in the hallway. Heather feels hurt, scared, and alone. She isn't ready to have a baby, and she doesn't know where to turn.

Kyle's and Heather's story is not unique. Depressants and other drugs change the way the mind works. They often affect people's judgment and make them careless. When people use drugs, they are more likely to do things that they wouldn't do if they were thinking clearly.

Recent studies found a direct link between the use of alcohol and other drugs and risky sexual behavior. Studies also show that young people are more likely to have unprotected sex after drinking alcohol than when they are sober. This unhealthy behavior puts preteens and teens at great risk for unplanned pregnancy, sexual assault, and sexually transmitted diseases, including AIDS.

HIV AND AIDS

Besides being linked to risky sexual behavior, HIV—the virus that causes AIDS—is spread through the sharing of hypodermic needles. Certain types of drugs, such as cocaine and heroin, are injected into the bloodstream with hypodermic needles. Health care professionals use a hypodermic needle only once and then throw it away. Drug users, however, sometimes share needles, and the needles become dirty and unsafe. If a drug user has HIV, another person sharing that needle will almost certainly become infected. HIV almost always turns into AIDS, and AIDS is usually fatal. That means you can die from AIDS. In fact, AIDS is the sixth leading cause of death among 15- to 20-year-olds in the United States (NCADI, 1997).

SUICIDE

There is no direct link between suicide, or taking one's own life, and the use of alcohol or other drugs. However, alcohol and drug use often contribute to the problem. Alcohol or drug use may impair the judgment of a person who is thinking about suicide. This may cause the person to act on his or her thoughts. Here is something you should know about suicide: Between 20 and 35 percent of people who committed suicide had been drinking shortly before they died, or had a history of alcohol abuse (NCADI, 1997).

DRUGS IN THE WORKPLACE

Kendra Washington's mother used to have a serious problem with crack. She was always getting high and often ended up being late for work or missing it completely. Kendra would have to call her mother's boss and make excuses. Mrs. Washington lost several jobs because of her addiction. A few months ago, Mrs. Washington's supervisor recognized that she had a drug problem. He helped Kendra's mother enter a drug rehab program, and today she is drug free. She is also a much more valuable employee.

Drugs in the workplace cause many problems and cost businesses billions of dollars each year. Employees who use drugs are much less productive and miss more work than other employees. They are also more likely to hurt themselves or their coworkers. For these reasons many companies have begun testing potential employees for drug use before they are hired.

DRUGS AND THE LAW

Jamal is only 16, but he looks older. One morning he made his usual stop at the convenience store to buy cigarettes. The new store owner asked to see some identification. As Jamal found out, it is illegal for anyone under the age of 18 to buy cigarettes in the United States.

TOBACCO

Even though most young people know about the harm caused by cigarettes, many continue to smoke. In the United States, nearly 3,000 young people become regular smokers each day. Between 1991 and 1995, the percentage of young people in grades eight to ten who smoke rose by nearly 35 percent.

To protect preteens and teens from the dangers of smoking, the government recently made stricter laws regarding the sale and advertising of tobacco. Here are some examples of the new laws:

▶ Store clerks must ask for photo identification from anyone who appears to be under the age of 27 who tries to buy cigarettes.

▶ Cigarette vending machines are banned except in places where only people over 18 are allowed, such as nightclubs.

The Story of Tim Allen

You may be wondering why a story about Tim Allen appears in a book about drug abuse. You probably know Tim Allen from television and the movies. He started out as a stand-up comic and now stars in his own hit television show, "Home Improvement." You probably also know that he has appeared in several popular

Tim Allen was very lucky to be able to turn his life around.

movies and has written some books. But what you may not know about Tim Allen is that he spent time in jail for selling drugs.

One of six children, Tim grew up in Denver, Colorado, and had a fairly typical childhood. When he was only 11 years old, however, tragedy struck. Tim's father was killed in a car accident. "My world changed overnight," Tim wrote in his first book.

A few years later, Tim's mother remarried, and the family moved to a suburb outside of Detroit, Michigan. Tim was not a great student in high school. His grades were barely good enough for him to make it into college. He did, however, earn a degree from Western Michigan University. Soon afterward Tim started hanging around with friends who used drugs. Tim became involved with drugs, too. Then, in 1979, he was arrested for selling cocaine.

Tim received an eight-year prison sentence. He served a little more than two years in jail, and the experience changed his life forever. "Prison takes away your freedom in a way you can never imagine until you've spent time there," Tim wrote. "Prison was the worst and the best thing that ever happened to me. It taught me in no uncertain terms to be responsible for my own actions."

In some ways Tim was lucky. His family supported him throughout his prison term. He and his college sweetheart married after his release from prison. Serving time in prison was probably the most difficult experience Tim ever faced. But he was able to turn his life around and kick his drug habit. Tim Allen learned that you don't need to use drugs to be happy and successful.

Stricter drug laws may prevent more young people from becoming involved in illegal and unhealthy activities.

▶ Billboards showing cigarette advertisements must be at least 1,000 feet away from schools and playgrounds.

▶ In magazines and other publications aimed at young people, tobacco advertising must be black and white—no color, and no pictures may be used to make the ads more attractive.

▶ Cigarette manufacturers are not allowed to sell or give away such items as T-shirts, baseball caps, mugs, and key chains that show product names or logos.

ALCOHOL

Marissa turned 17 a few months ago. As soon as she got her driver's license, she bought a used car with money she had saved from years of baby-sitting. One night Marissa went to a party at a friend's house. Everyone at the party was drinking, and Marissa had a few beers.

As Marissa was driving home that night, she lost control of her car while going around a curve. She slammed on the brakes but couldn't stop from hitting a parked car. Marissa was scared and shaken up, but not hurt. When the police arrived, they asked her to take a breath test. The test showed that Marissa had been drinking.

Marissa was very lucky. She wasn't hurt, and she didn't hurt anyone else. However, she had to go to court, and she may lose her driver's license. She must also pay for the damage done to both her own car and the parked car she hit.

In all states except Louisiana, drinking alcohol is illegal for anyone under the age of 21. And driving while under the influence of alcohol is always illegal, no matter how old you are or what state you live in.

OTHER DRUGS

You have probably seen headlines like the following in the newspaper or heard similar stories on radio or television:

Athlete Tests Positive for Steroids;
Banned from Competition

Movie Star Arrested for Cocaine Possession;
Will Spend Time in Jail

Rock Star Overdoses on Heroin;
In Hospital for Rehab

You may also know of young people who have been caught using drugs. They may have been kicked off a sports team, expelled from school, or made to complete a drug treatment program. In some cases, they may even have gone to jail.

Besides tobacco and alcohol, most of the drugs you have learned about in this book are illegal for anyone to use, not just people under the age of 18. These drugs include marijuana, cocaine, crack, and LSD. A few drugs, such as stimulants and depressants, are legal when prescribed by a physician and taken only as directed by the doctor.

The penalties for drug possession vary, depending on such factors as state laws, age of the user, type of drug used, and prior drug offenses. For some drugs, even a first offense can result in a jail sentence. And the penalties for selling drugs are even tougher than those for possessing them.

STAYING DRUG FREE

Serena recently moved to a new town. She was pretty nervous about going to a new school. Because Serena was shy, it took a while for her to make friends.

By the end of her first week at school, Serena had met only a few people. Then, during lunch one Friday, Jennifer motioned for Serena to sit with her and some of her friends. Jennifer was one of the most popular girls in school. She invited Serena to come over to her house after school. Serena was thrilled.

When Serena arrived at Jennifer's house, several other girls were already there. Jennifer's parents weren't home, and the girls were playing loud music. Jennifer came out of the bathroom with a couple of bottles of nail polish remover. She poured the liquid onto some rags and put the rags in plastic bags. Then she handed one of the bags to Serena.

"What's this for?" asked Serena. She was starting to feel nervous and scared.

"Haven't you ever tried huffing before?" asked Jennifer. "Just breathe it in. It'll give you a great rush!"

"No, thanks," said Serena. "I'm not into drugs. Why don't we do something else instead?

"Come on," said Jennifer, "don't be such a baby. This is fun, and it won't hurt you."

Walking away from your friends may be hard, but it is even harder to walk away from drug addiction.

"That's OK," said Serena. "I think I'd better go." As she walked toward the door, tears welled up in her eyes. She felt the other girls staring at her and heard them whispering. But once she was outside, she felt relieved. Making new friends wasn't worth doing something she would regret later.

SAYING NO TO DRUGS

Although it was very difficult, Serena made the right decision. She knew that using inhalants was wrong and could be harmful. She suggested other activities that didn't involve drugs. When that didn't work, the only thing left to do was walk away. It took a lot of courage for her to do that.

During adolescence you may face a lot of peer pressure. Like Serena, you may find yourself in a difficult situation in which other people are encouraging you to use drugs. Resisting peer pressure is not easy, but kicking a drug habit is much harder. When you say no to drugs, you are staying in control of the situation, making your own decisions, and acting responsibly. And you can feel very proud of yourself for doing so.

SEEKING HELP

If you or someone you know already has a drug problem, it is not too late to seek help. There is no shame attached to admitting that a problem exists or to asking for help. It is, above all, necessary to recognize that something serious has happened and that it needs attention. Most drug users can't recover on their own. Talking to a trusted adult, or calling a toll-free drug hot line are ways to begin to get the needed help.

Although people with drug addictions, including alcohol addiction, can be treated, they will always have the tendency to become addicted again. For as long as they remain drug free, they will be "in recovery" from their addiction. And they must never again use the drug to which they are addicted—or any other drug, unless it is prescribed by a physician.

BENEFITS OF STAYING DRUG FREE

As stated earlier, it is much easier to say no to drugs now than to break a drug habit later. There are also many other reasons to avoid tobacco, alcohol, and other drugs. People who don't use drugs:

- Have better relationships with family and friends
- Feel more energetic and alert
- Are able to concentrate and think clearly
- Earn better grades in school
- Look better and feel healthier
- Are in control of their feelings and actions
- Perform better in sports and other activities
- Make smarter choices
- Have more money (because they don't spend it on drugs)
- Live longer, happier lives

TAKING RESPONSIBILITY

By reading this book, you have taken an important step toward a healthy, drug-free life. You have informed yourself about drug abuse. Now you know the dangers involved.

If you have become addicted to drugs and want to overcome the addiction, or if a friend needs help with an addiction, you know what to do. It takes a special kind of courage to recognize that you have a serious problem. Going through detox may be physically and emotionally difficult, but the time it takes to rid your body of harmful drugs is short when compared to the rest of your life. The responsibility is yours alone. Don't let another day go by without helping yourself (or a friend). The time to act is now!

addict: Person who has an uncontrollable physical or mental need for a substance.

addiction: Unhealthy and uncontrollable dependence on a substance, such as alcohol or another drug.

amphetamine: Drug that stimulates, or speeds up, the nervous system.

depressant: Drug, such as alcohol, that slows down the functioning of the brain and relaxes muscles.

detox: Short for *detoxification,* which means "ridding the body of harmful substances."

drug abuse: Using drugs in ways that are illegal or unhealthy.

hallucinogen: Drug that produces visions of things that are not really there, or sounds that are not real.

inhalant: Drug that is inhaled, or breathed, into the lungs.

narcotic: Drug that produces sleepiness and reduces pain by dulling the senses.

physical dependence: Type of addiction in which a user's body needs the drug in order to function.

prescription medication: Drugs available in a pharmacy only with a physician's written permission.

psychological dependence: Type of addiction in which a drug user believes that he or she needs the drug.

rehab: Short for *rehabilitation,* which means "restoring to good health."

steroids: Group of powerful drugs that mimic the effects of hormones, which are chemical substances in the body that regulate many body functions.

stimulant: Type of drug that increases brain activity and makes a person more alert.

symptom: Noticeable change in the body that indicates illness.

tolerance: Condition in which the body adapts to the effects of a drug and needs a greater amount to achieve the same effect.

withdrawal: Unpleasant mental and physical symptoms that occur when a drug user stops using the drug.

WHERE TO GO FOR HELP

Support Groups and Hot Lines

Al-Anon and Alateen
Look in your telephone directory
for local listings.

Alcoholics Anonymous (AA)
Look in your telephone directory
for local listings.

Cocaine Helpline
(800) COCAINE

National Drug and Alcohol
Treatment Referral Service
(800) 662-HELP
(800) 66-AYUDA (Spanish)

National Organizations

American Council for
Drug Education
164 West 74th Street
New York, NY 10023
(800) 488-3784

Mothers Against Drunk Driving
(MADD)
511 East John Carpenter Freeway,
Suite 700
Irving, TX 75062
(214) 744-6233

Narcotics Anonymous
World Service Office
P.O. Box 9999
Van Nuys, CA 91409
(818) 773-9999

National Clearinghouse for
Alcohol and Drug Information
P.O. Box 2345
Rockville, MD 20847-2345
(800) 729-6686
http://www.health.org (website)

National Council on Alcoholism
and Drug Dependence
12 West 21st Street, 7th Floor
New York, NY 10010
(800) 622-2255

Parents Resource Institute for
Drug Education (PRIDE)
The Hurt Building
50 Hurt Plaza, Suite 210
Atlanta, GA 30303
(800) 241-7946

Canadian Organizations

Canadian Centre on
Substance Abuse
#300, 75 Albert Street
Ottawa, ON K1P 5E7
(613) 235-4048

Council on Drug Abuse
#17, 698 Weston Road
Toronto, ON M6N 3R3
(416) 763-1491

International Development
Research Center
P.O. Box 8500
Ottawa, ON
Canada K1G3H9

Narcotics Anonymous
P.O. Box 5700
Toronto, ON M5W 1N8
(416) 691-9519

FOR MORE INFORMATION

Books

Ball, Jacqueline A. *Everything You Need to Know About Drug Abuse.* The Need to Know Library. Rosen, 1994.

Cheney, Glenn Alan. *Drugs, Teens, and Recovery: Real-Life Stories of Trying to Stay Clean.* Enslow, 1993.

Friedman, David. *Focus on Drugs and the Brain.* A Drug-Alert Book. Twenty-First Century, 1990.

Hermes, William J. *Substance Abuse.* The Encyclopedia of Health. Chelsea House, 1993.

Hyde, Margaret O. *Know About Drugs,* 4th ed. New York: Walker and Company, 1996.

———. *Know About Smoking,* 3rd ed. New York: Walker and Company, 1995.

Langone, John. *Tough Choices: A Book About Substance Abuse.* Little, Brown and Company, 1995.

Myers, Arthur. *Drugs and Peer Pressure.* The Drug Abuse Prevention Library. Rosen, 1995.

Phillips, Lynn. *Drug Abuse.* Life Issues. Marshall Cavendish, 1994.

Salak, John. *Drugs in Society: Are They Our Suicide Pill?* Twenty-First Century, 1993.

Wax, Wendy. *Say No and Know Why: Kids Learn About Drugs.* Walker and Company, 1992.

Wijnberg, Ellen. *Alcohol.* Teen Hot Line Series. Raintree Steck-Vaughn, 1994.

Other Sources

Drugs of Abuse. U.S. Department of Justice, Drug Enforcement Administration, 1996.

Marijuana: Facts for Teens. National Institute on Drug Abuse, 1996.

Straight Facts About Drugs and Alcohol. National Clearinghouse for Alcohol and Drug Information, 1997.

Tips for Teens. National Clearinghouse for Alcohol and Drug Information, 1997.

INDEX